My Path to Math

123456789

PATTERNING

Minta Berry

Crabtree Publishing Company

www.crabtreebooks.com

Author: Minta Berry
Editor: Reagan Miller
Proofreader: Crystal Sikkens
Cover design: Margaret Amy Salter
Editorial director: Kathy Middleton
Production coordinator: Margaret Amy Salter
Prepress technician: Ken Wright
Print coordinator: Katherine Berti
Project manager: Kirsten Holm, Shivi Sharma (Planman Technologies)
Photo research: Iti Shrotriya (Planman Technologies)
Technical art: Arka Roy Chaudhary (Planman Technologies)

Photographs:
Cover: monkeybusinessimages/BigStockPhoto (c), Beata Becla/Shutterstock (br); P4: (t) PhotoHappiness/Shutterstock, PhotoHappiness/Shutterstock; (b) 4ever.Rik/Shutterstock; P5: Thomas Northcut/Thinkstock; P6: (t) Alexpi/Shutterstock, (b) George Filyagin/Shutterstock; P7: Hxdbzxy/Shutterstock; P9: Hxdbzxy/Shutterstock; P10: (t) Matka Wariatka/Fotolia, (b) Matka Wariatka/Fotolia; P11: (bkgd) Brand X Pictures/Thinkstock, (fgd) Matka Wariatka/Fotolia; P12: Comstock/Thinkstock; P13: (t) Ryan McVay/Thinkstock; (b) Steve Cukrov/Shutterstock; P14: (l) Eric Isselée/Shutterstock, (c) JinYoung Lee/Shutterstock, (r) Gracious Tiger/Shutterstock; P 15: (l) Eric Isselée/Shutterstock, (cl) JinYoung Lee/Shutterstock, (cr) Gracious Tiger/Shutterstock, (r) Talvi/Shutterstock; P16: Alexander Kalina/Shutterstock; P17: (bkgd) Stasys Eidiejus/123RF, (fgd) Sukiyaki/Shutterstock; P19: Robert Aubin/Bigstock; P21: Nils Z/Shutterstock; P23: (t) Alexpi/Shutterstock; (b) Steve Cukrov/Shutterstock.
(t = top, b = bottom, l = left, c= center, r = right, bkgd = background, fgd = foreground)

Library and Archives Canada Cataloguing in Publication

Berry, Minta
      Patterning / Minta Berry.

(My path to math)
Includes index.
Issued also in electronic formats.
ISBN 978-0-7787-5278-3 (bound).--ISBN 978-0-7787-5267-7 (pbk.)

      1. Sequences (Mathematics)--Juvenile literature. 2. Pattern perception--Juvenile literature. I. Title. II. Series: My path to math

QA292.B47 2011   j515'.24   C2011-907556-3

Library of Congress Cataloging-in-Publication Data

Berry, Minta.
   Patterning / Minta Berry.
      p. cm. -- (My path to math)
   Includes index.
   ISBN 978-0-7787-5278-3 (reinforced library binding : alk. paper) -- ISBN 978-0-7787-5267-7 (pbk. : alk. paper) -- ISBN 978-1-4271-8808-3 (electronic pdf) -- ISBN 978-1-4271-9649-1 (electronic html)
   1. Sequences (Mathematics)--Juvenile literature. 2. Pattern perception--Juvenile literature. I. Title.

QA292.B47 2012
515'.24--dc23
                                                    2011040396

Crabtree Publishing Company

www.crabtreebooks.com   1-800-387-7650

Printed in the U.S.A./112011/JA20111018

Published in Canada
Crabtree Publishing
616 Welland Ave.
St. Catharines, ON
L2M 5V6

Published in the United States
Crabtree Publishing
PMB 59051
350 Fifth Avenue, 59th Floor
New York, New York 10118

Published in the United Kingdom
Crabtree Publishing
Maritime House
Basin Road North, Hove
BN41 1WR

Published in Australia
Crabtree Publishing
3 Charles Street
Coburg North
VIC 3058

Contents

What Is a Pattern?

Jackson looks for **patterns** every day. A pattern is a set of things that repeat over and over again. Our world is filled with patterns!

This pattern has two red socks and one blue sock. The pattern keeps going.

We can make patterns with many things. We can make patterns with objects like socks. We can make patterns with numbers and shapes. Patterns do not have to be things we can see. Patterns can be sounds we can hear.

Activity Box

Look at the marbles. What is the pattern?

Jackson sees his brother Allan. Allan's shirt has a striped pattern. His shirt has orange stripes and brown stripes.

Repeating Patterns

Jackson goes to the kitchen to get a snack. He sees more patterns there. Red and green apples make a **repeating pattern**. One green apple and one red apple make a **pattern core**. Jackson uses the pattern core to make a repeating pattern.

1	2	3

Jackson repeats his pattern core three times.

Activity Box

Look at the pattern below. What is the pattern core? How many times does it repeat?

Jackson makes repeating patterns with cups. His first repeating pattern has a pattern core of one pink cup and one blue cup.

Jackson uses the cups to make another pattern. This pattern core is two pink cups and one blue cup.

Extend a Repeating Pattern

Jackson, Michael, and Serika go to a pet store. The owner shows them turtles and snakes. He gives them stamps of these animals. Serika uses the stamps to make a repeating pattern.

 **?**

Serika asks Jackson to add the next stamp. Jackson adds a turtle to **extend** the pattern. To extend the pattern is to continue the pattern and make it longer.

Activity Box

Look at each pattern. What comes next to extend the pattern?

Jackson, Serika, and Michael learn about animals at the zoo.

Serika makes a pattern core.

Serika extends the pattern core.

Serika extends the pattern core again.

Geometric Patterns

Jackson is making a pattern by building towers with blocks at daycare. He chooses the blocks below to be elements in his pattern.

An **element** is each object in a pattern. Jackson uses six elements in his pattern.

Next, Jackson puts together the pattern core. Which element does he use twice?

Jackson makes a pattern with blocks. Then he extends the pattern. How many times does he repeat the pattern core?

Activity Box

Draw this pattern on a piece of paper.

- What elements are in the pattern?
- Circle the pattern core.
- Extend the pattern by adding the next three elements.

Growing Patterns

Jackson goes bowling with his Uncle Liam. They have fun bowling together. Jackson sees a pattern in the bowling pins.

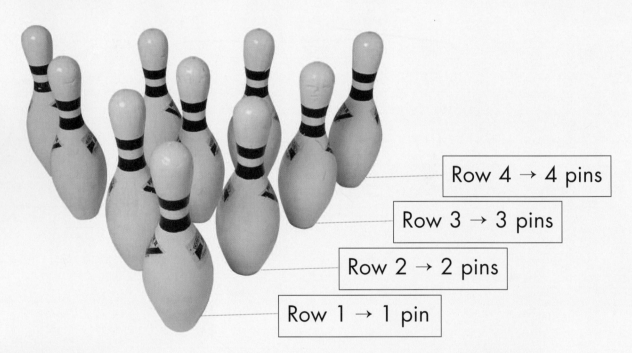

Row 4 → 4 pins

Row 3 → 3 pins

Row 2 → 2 pins

Row 1 → 1 pin

Bowling pins are set in a **growing pattern**. Each row grows larger by one more pin.

Activity Box

Look at the pattern below. Which shape is growing? How is it growing?

Jackson sets up his toy bowling pins at home. The pins are in a growing pattern. They grow by one.

Extend a Growing Pattern

Jackson goes to the zoo with his dad. They see many kinds of animals. Jackson counts the animals. He sees a growing pattern.

1 monkey   2 zebras   3 tigers

Next, Jackson visits the elephants. If his growing pattern continues, how many elephants would he see? You are right! He sees four elephants.

First Jackson saw one monkey. Then he saw two zebras. Next he saw three tigers. Then he saw four elephants. The number of animals is growing by one.

Here are two more ways to show the same growing pattern.

The pattern grows by one animal.

Activity Box

Look at this growing pattern. How does the pattern grow?

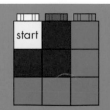

Draw the pattern. Add purple cubes to grow the pattern.

Repeating Patterns in Our Lives

On Fridays Jackson visits a new place with his scout troop. This Friday he will visit the fire station. Next Friday he will go to the recycling center.

Jackson looks at a calendar. He sees a repeating pattern in the days of the week. He circles Friday.

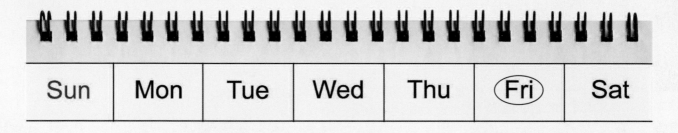

Sun	Mon	Tue	Wed	Thu	Fri	Sat

Every week has the same seven days. The seven days make up the pattern core.

May

S	M	Tu	W	Th	F	S
				1	2	3
4	5	6	7	8	9	10
11	12	13	14	15	16	17
18	19	20	21	22	23	24
25	26	27	28	29	30	31

June

July

S	M	Tu	W	Th	F
		1	2	3	4
6	7	8	9	10	11
13	14	15	16	17	18
20	21	22	23	24	25
27	28	29	30	31	

Sunday	Monday	Tuesday	Wednesday	Thursday	Friday	Saturday
2	3	4	5	6	7	
9	10	11	12	13 FIRE STATION	14	
16	17	18	19	20 RECYCLING CENTER	21	
23	24	25	26	27		
30						

Mom writes Jackson's scout troop trips on the calendar. Jackson looks forward to Fridays.

Activity Box

If today is Monday, what day will it be tomorrow?

If today is Thursday, what day was it yesterday?

What days of the week do you go to school?

Are there other activities you do every week?

Make a calendar for this month and write your activities on it.

Create Repeating Patterns

Marley is Jackson's sister. Jackson shows Marley how to make a repeating pattern. He draws a chalk pattern at the playground. Marley tries to make the same pattern.

○ △△ → ○ △△ → ○ △△ →   .... Jackson's pattern

○ △ → ○ △ → ○ △ → ○ △ →   .... Marley's pattern

Are the patterns the same? What is Jackson's pattern core?
Look at the △.
Jackson uses two △ in his pattern. Marley uses only one △.

Activity Box

Clap your hands and stomp your feet to make a repeating pattern. Try these patterns first.

clap clap stomp   stomp stomp stomp clap
clap clap stomp   stomp stomp stomp clap
clap clap stomp   stomp stomp stomp clap
clap clap stomp

Look at the shape of the hopscotch court. Do you see a pattern? See how the pattern repeats. What is the pattern core?

Create Growing Patterns

Tables are a good way to see growing patterns. Jackson is going to the recycling center. He wants to recycle cans.

Jackson saves cans for five weeks. At the end of each week, Jackson counts the number of cans he has saved. He writes the number of cans on his table.

How does the number of cans grow each week? It grows by two cans each week.

Week	Cans
1	4
2	6
3	8
4	10
5	12

Week	Cans	
1	4	> 2
2	6	> 2
3	8	> 2
4	10	> 2
5	12	

Activity Box

Extend the table. If Jackson continues his growing pattern, how many cans will Jackson have in week 6?

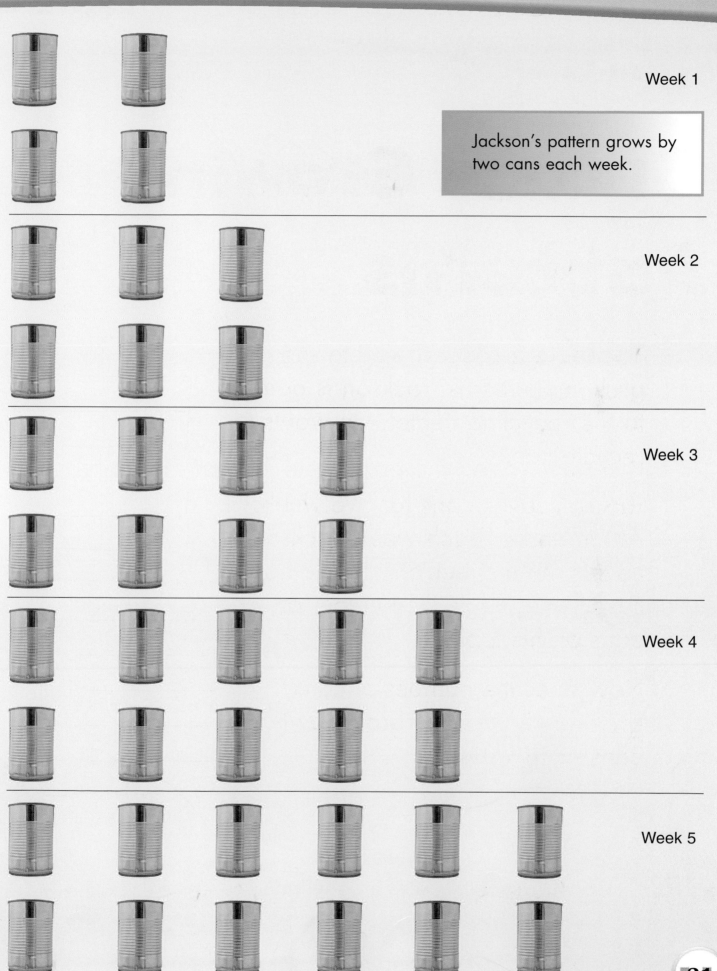

Week 1

Jackson's pattern grows by two cans each week.

Week 2

Week 3

Week 4

Week 5

21

Glossary

element Each object in a pattern

extend To add the next object to keep the pattern going

growing pattern Pattern that gets bigger

pattern core The part of the pattern that repeats

pattern A set of things that repeats over and over again

repeating pattern Using the same pattern core again and again

table A way to organize information that makes it easy to compare

element

pattern core

repeating pattern

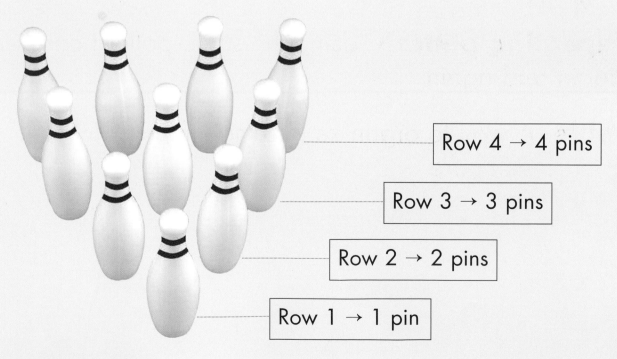

Row 4 → 4 pins

Row 3 → 3 pins

Row 2 → 2 pins

Row 1 → 1 pin

growing pattern

Index